JACKSON BROWNE
THE

MW00576473

Project Manager: Carol Cuellar
Book Artwork Layout: Martha L. Ramirez
Album Artwork © 2002 Elektra Entertainment Group, Inc.
Album Artwork: Dustin Stanton
Photography: Nels Israelson and Dianna Cohen
Publishing Administration: Randall Wixen
Management: Donald Miller, Cree Clover

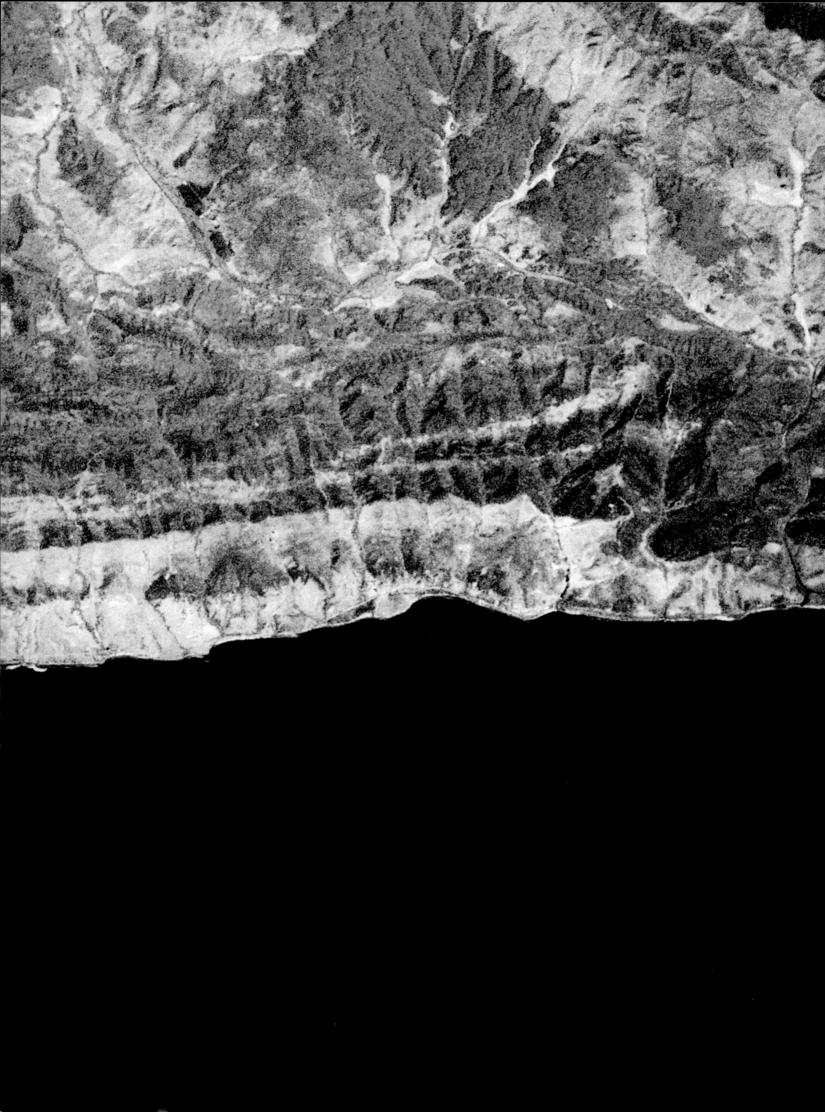

THE NAKED RIDE HOME

Gtr. tuned down 1/2 step:
⑥ = Eb ③ = Gb
⑤ = Ab ② = Bb
④ = Db ① = Eb

Words and Music by
JACKSON BROWNE

1. "Just take off your clothes, and I'll___ drive you home,"___ I said,
2. 3. 5. *See additional lyrics*
4. *(Inst. solo ad lib....*

The Naked Ride Home - 5 - 1
PFM0323

8

Chorus:
1. 4.
2. 3. 5.
D A
D♭ A♭
... end solo)
On that free - way, the light
G D A G
G♭ D♭ A♭ G♭
was re - ceed - ing. Her beau - ty, a sight so mis - lead - ing. I
D A G A
D♭ A♭ G♭ A♭
failed to hear the heart that was beat - ing a - lone

on the na - ked___ ride___ home.

(Inst. solo ad lib....

... end solo)

Inst. solo ad lib.

10

Verse 2:
My eyes on the road, she slid herself down in the seat,
And a vision of paradise swung into view.
Across those five lanes, not one driver glanced over to see
The beauty known only to me, and a big rig or two.
(To Chorus:)

Verse 3:
With the trace of a smile and that defiant look in her eye,
She hurtled through space in a world of her own.
And turning aside my caress, spoke of all that she'd not yet done,
As if I was the doubting one who would have to be shown.
(To Chorus:)

Verse 4:
(Instrumental solo)

Verse 5:
She gathered her clothes and ran through the yard in the dark,
Up onto the porch like a flash, and inside.
Then one room at a time, I watched every light in our house come on,
Like the truth that would eventually dawn, forcing me to decide.
(To Chorus:)

THE NIGHT INSIDE ME

Lyrics by JACKSON BROWNE
Music by JACKSON BROWNE, KEVIN McCORMICK,
MARK GOLDENBERG, MAURICIO LEWAK and JEFF YOUNG

Moderately fast rock ♩ = 152

1. I used to lay out in a field un-der the Milk-y Way___
2.3. *See additional lyrics*

with ev-'ry-thing that I was feel-ing that I could not say,___

with ev - 'ry doubt and ev - 'ry

sor - row that was in my way___

tear-ing a - round in - side my head like it was there to stay.___

Chorus:

1. Night in my___ eyes, the night in - side_
2.3. *See additional lyrics*

The Night Inside Me - 7 - 4
PFM0323

16

D.S. 𝄋 al Coda

The Night Inside Me - 7 - 6
PFM0323

Repeat ad lib. and fade

Verse 2:
I caught a ride into the city every chance I got.
I wasn't sure there was a name for the life I sought.
Now I'm a long way gone down the life I got.
I don't know how I believed some of the things I thought.

Chorus 2:
Night in my eyes, the night inside me,
Here where the shadows gather to decide me.
Night in my eyes,
Out at the end of light and gravity,
Waiting for night.
(To Guitar solo:)

Verse 3:
I walk around inside the questions of my day.
I navigate the inner reaches of my disarray.
I pass the altars where fools and thieves hold sway.
I wait for the night to come and lift this dread away.

Chorus 3:
Night in my eyes, the night inside me,
Here where the shadows and the light divide me.
Night in my eyes,
Night full of promise and uncertainty,
Waiting for the night to set me free.

CASINO NATION

Lyrics by JACKSON BROWNE
Music by JACKSON BROWNE, KEVIN McCORMICK,
MARK GOLDENBERG, MAURICIO LEWAK and JEFF YOUNG

Moderately ♩ = 69

1. 2.

3.

2nd time - Drum fill

Verses 1 & 2:

Am7(4)

1. In a wea-pons pro-duc-ing na-tion un-der Je - sus,__
2. *See additional lyrics*

in the fa-bled cru - ci-ble__ of the free world,_

cam-'ra crews search__ for clues__ a-mid the de - tri-tus

24

Verse 2:
Gleaming faces in the check-out counter at the Church of Fame,
The lucky winners cheer Casino Nation.
All those not on T V only have themselves to blame,
And don't quite seem to understand
The way the hammer shapes the hand.
(To Bridge:)

FOR TAKING THE TROUBLE

Words and Music by
JACKSON BROWNE

* "Drop D" tuning for recorded guitar arranged in standard tuning.

For Taking the Trouble - 7 - 1
PFM0323

Chorus:

Tears of laugh-ter, tears of grief;__ are they the tears of a cap-tured_ thief?_

You thought that you were home___ free. You thought you had her
You're learn-in' how to talk a-bout it. You're learn-in' how to

well__ in hand, but there were things a-bout her you did-n't un-der-stand._
bend._ It's like you're learn-in' how to walk all o-ver a-gain.__

Chorus:

Inst. solo ad lib.

NEVER STOP

Lyrics by JACKSON BROWNE
Music by JACKSON BROWNE, KEVIN McCORMICK,
MARK GOLDENBERG, MAURICIO LEWAK and JEFF YOUNG

* "Drop D" tuning for recorded guitar arranged in standard tuning.

34

Bridge:

world_ has been show - ing_ you how_ it's no place for_ your ten - der_ heart_

_ now. In a world that_ keeps_ turn - ing_ you down,_ on - ly the heart_

_ knows_ where the strength can be found._

D.S. ℅ al Coda

Coda

Re - mem - ber when_ you look in - to my

Never Stop - 8 - 6
PFM0323

37

Verse 2:
And I remember how you helped me, baby,
And all the times you had my back.
And how you wrapped me in your sweetness,
And held my eyes with your eyes when my train was off the track.
Now I got some things that I want to do, and I want to do them with you,
If you'll just stand by me, and don't look back.
(To Chorus:)

40

WALKING TOWN

Lyrics by JACKSON BROWNE
Music by JACKSON BROWNE, KEVIN McCORMICK,
MARK GOLDENBERG, MAURICIO LEWAK and JEFF YOUNG

Gtr. tuned down 1/2 step:
⑥ = E♭   ③ = G♭
⑤ = A♭   ② = B♭
④ = D♭   ① = E♭

Moderate funk beat ♩ = 96

Walking Town - 7 - 1
PFM0323

42

To Next Strain

Out here where the days go by, and the
Stressed out in the lat - est style; how

glanc - es nev - er meet_ the eye.__ It's a
long has it been since you walked_ a mile

in yours or an - y - bod - y els - e's shoes?_

Well, in an - y life,_ there will be dues._ It's a

Walking Town - 7 - 3
PFM0323

Walk-in' up,___ walk-in' down,__ walk-in' back,__ walk-in' 'round.__

Walk-in' mute,__ walk-in' bound,__ walk-in' though__ your walk-in' town.__

Solo:

(Inst. solo ad lib....

Walking Town - 7 - 5
PFM0323

ABOUT MY IMAGINATION

Lyrics by JACKSON BROWNE
Music by JACKSON BROWNE, KEVIN McCORMICK,
MARK GOLDENBERG, MAURICIO LEWAK and JEFF YOUNG

Moderately slow rock shuffle ♩ = 76

1. I kept my eyes___ o-pen and tried___ to see___
2. 3. *See additional lyrics*

the point of what___ went on___ in front of me.___

Chorus 1:

1. A - bout my i - mag - i - na - tion, got me through some - how.

With - out my i - mag - i - na - tion, would - n't be here now.

Electric Piano solo:

Verse 2:
It's been so hard sometimes to find my way.
I let my pleasure lead my little world astray.
And if I'm truthful I'll say that I was blind
To everything about this life but what I had in mind
And it was easy then to say where love could go
It's so easy when there's so much you don't know.
(To Chorus 1:)

Verse 3:
I keep my eyes open and try to see
This life in terms of possibility.
With so much changing, and changing for the worse,
You got to keep your head up, baby,
From the cradle to the hearse.
And it was easy then to say where love could go.
It's so easy when love is all you know.
(To Chorus 3:)

SERGIO LEONE

Lyrics by JACKSON BROWNE
Music by JACKSON BROWNE, KEVIN McCORMICK,
MARK GOLDENBERG, MAURICIO LEWAK and JEFF YOUNG

Moderately ♩ = 112

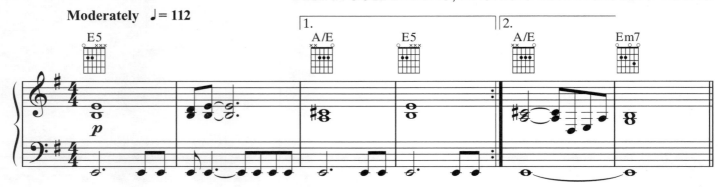

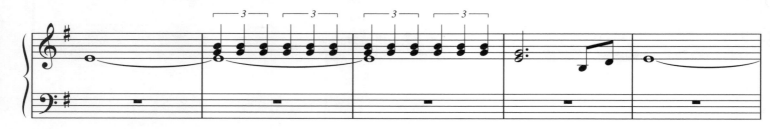

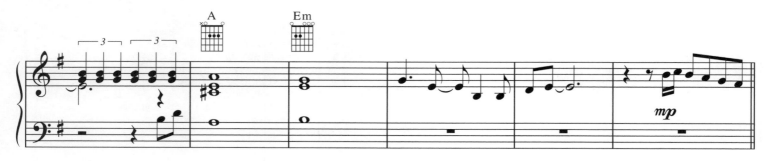

60

Verse 3:

3. He worked for Walsh and Wy - ler with___ the char - i - ot___ and sword. When he rode out___ in the des - ert he___ was quot-ing Hawks and Ford.___ He came to see___ the mas-

62

64

Repeat ad lib. and fade

Verse 2:
He could see the killer's faces and he heard the song they sang
Where he waited in the darkness with the Viale Glorioso gang.
He could see the blood approaching and he knew what he would be
Since the days when he was first assisting The Force Of Destiny.

MY STUNNING MYSTERY COMPANION

Moderately ♩ = 96

Words and Music by
JACKSON BROWNE

What with all___ my ex-pec-ta-tions long a-ban-doned, and a fu-

ture I___ no long-er saw my hand in, how I found you is be-yond___ my un-der-stand-

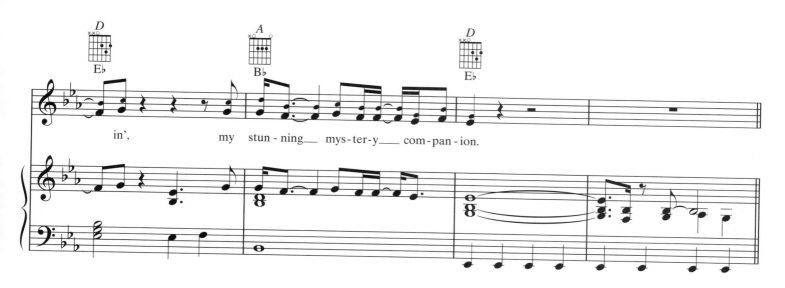

in', my stun-ning___ mys-ter-y___ com-pan-ion.

© 2002 Swallow Turn Music (ASCAP)
All Rights Administered by WIXEN MUSIC PUBLISHING INC.
All Rights Reserved

67

where we could slow down,__ and you could put a lit-tle more_ work in on me.

1. 3.   To Next Strain   2.   D.S. %   Chorus:

What with all__   ...end solo)   __ my ex-pec-ta-tions long a-ban-

doned,   my sol-i-tar-y na-ture not__ with-stand-ing,   you're__ the

one who pulled me out__ of that__ crash land-in',
doubt that you're the rea-son I'm__ still stand-in',   my stun-ning___ mys-ter-y___ com-pan-

My Stunning Mystery Companion - 5 - 3
PFM0323

68

ion.

ion.

Solo Verse:

Inst. solo ad lib.

Repeat ad lib. and fade

Verse 3:
Right now, I can't quite remember
The cause of all my tears.
I hear you laughing, and somehow
The past just disappears.
Maybe you were joking when you said
You'd take me for ten years and no more.
Maybe you've had the best of me,
But you could take another ten years and be sure.
(To Chorus:)

DON'T YOU WANT TO BE THERE?

Words and Music by
JACKSON BROWNE

71

Don't You Want to Be There? - 6 - 2
PFM0323

73

Don't You Want to Be There? - 6 - 4
PFM0323

Verse 2:
Don't you want to be there, don't you want to fly?
With your arms out, let a shout take you across the sky
Don't you want to be there when the time's gone by?
(To Chorus 1:)

Verse 3:
Don't you want to be there?
Don't you want to know
Where the grace and simple truth of childhood go?
Don't you want to be there when the trumpets blow?

Chorus 2:
Blow for those born into hunger.
Blow for those lost 'neath the train.
Blow for those choking in anger.
Blow for those driven insane.
And those you have wronged, you know
You need to let them know some way.
And those who have wronged you,
Know you'll have to let them go someday.
Don't you want to be there? (Be there.)
Don't you want to see where the angels appear?
Don't you want to be where there's strength and love
In the place of fear?